This Journal Belongs To

____

____

Grateful Mother of

____

____

____

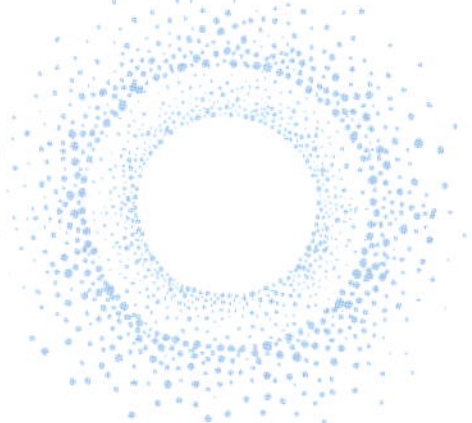

Introduction

We're Meagan and Sarah, the hosts and creators of *The Mom Hour* podcast, and we're grateful that you've picked up this journal.

As mothers with eight kids between us, we know exactly what it's like to feel like your life is consumed with wiping sticky fingers, cutting crusts off sandwiches, and picking up toys. In this messy and often monotonous stage of life, traditional journaling can feel repetitive ("pushed the stroller through the park today—again") and overwhelming ("where to begin? this is really, really hard"). And amid those endless nursing sessions or requests of "read it again, Mommy!" gratitude can often be hard to find.

Yet we also know that mothers want to find joy and meaning in the small moments. We want to capture those memories—funny and joyful and even frustrating—as they happen, in order to capture the essence of those long days and swiftly flying years and to remind ourselves that *yes, we were here,* and *yes, what we did mattered.*

With thoughtful prompts, this journal will help you create a record of not only *what* happened—exciting and exasperating moments alike—but *how you felt* about it. In short, this journal contains bite-size entries that are easy to fit into the margins of motherhood.

In our experience, the first step toward finding gratitude for all we experience as moms, is by giving ourselves the gift of noticing—and the space to learn as we go. By reflecting on ordinary days and extraordinary moments alike in these pages, using this journal will be a gift you give yourself: an opportunity to both celebrate small wins and acknowledge the hard stuff without the pressure to write it ALL down, every day.

We know you're busy making memories and you know just how fast these moments fly. We've created this journal to help you capture the essence of the season you're in and find the gratitude that comes with noticing life as it happens.

HOW TO USE THIS BOOK

The short answer: however you like! We know that traditional journaling can feel loaded with pressure to be thoughtful, poetic, and most of all, part of a consistent, daily practice. We also know that as moms, piling on that kind of expectation just leads to feeling overwhelmed. So while it may feel rebellious to "skip around" in a journal, we've purposefully designed this book to be flexible and dynamic, and to encourage you to flip through the pages to find a prompt that sparks something in you—whether that's every day, or just whenever you feel like it.

Feel free to jump around and be as inconsistent as life allows, and feel free to allow for space and time to elapse between sessions. We think that just cracking open the cover and thumbing through the pages a couple of times per week to see what prompts catch your eye is plenty. Or maybe you'll make it a monthly ritual by stealing away to a coffee shop or curling up after bedtime with this journal and a pen. There's no one right way, and no requirement. As long as you remember to jot the date down every time you fill out a page or respond to a prompt, you'll be able to remember later where you were in life when you captured that moment.

In the pages ahead, you'll find three separate sections, each with its own suggestions for how it can be used. Again, take our guidance as a suggestion only. This book is yours to use however it fits into your mom-life. However you use it, we hope it helps you notice, celebrate, and remember those moments with all the gratitude you can muster (and to give yourself a lot of grace when you're not feeling so celebratory).

Warmly,
Meagan and Sarah

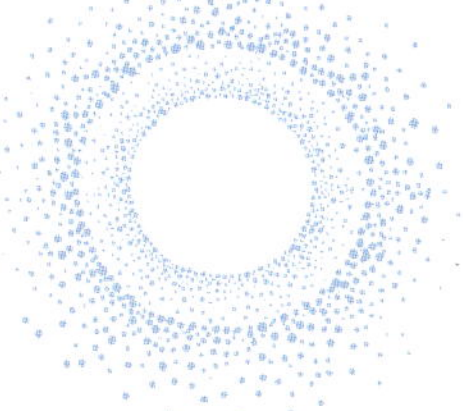

PART ONE

A Day In The Life

Capture a snapshot of where your motherhood life is right now by noticing—and noting—the small details that make up an ordinary day.

Cultivating a gratitude practice often centers around an awareness of the big stuff: our health, a roof over our heads, enough food to eat, and safety for our children and loved ones. And while remembering to be thankful for these fundamental gifts is important, we've found that noticing small, specific, and even frivolous things we're grateful for helps to sustain a gratitude practice.

Motherhood serves up plenty of challenges, disappointments, anxieties, and curveballs—and it's easy to focus more on the negative than the positive. But it's also true that, for many of us, a busy, chaotic life raising kids represents a life we once dreamed about. We think there's a balance to be found in acknowledging what's hard *and* identifying small things we're grateful for.

What better way to pay attention to those small moments and little joys than to reflect on an ordinary day in your motherhood life? This section includes 24 pages where you can capture a snapshot of a single day. It may not seem like anything special as you jot down your answers, but we think you'll find as you build this record of ordinary days that you're bringing awareness to what's good right now—even during the messiest of seasons.

How to Use This Section

We've included 12 Day in the Life templates in this section, with the idea that you fill one out somewhere between once per month and once per quarter—about 4–6 times per year. Maybe you'll create a monthly ritual where you sit down with a cup of tea on the same evening each month to journal about that day. Or maybe you'll open to this section more spontaneously, whenever the mood strikes. Either way, remember we're celebrating the small, the simple, and the very ordinary details of motherhood in these pages, so don't feel like you need anything spectacular to report!

A Day In The Life

DATE ____/____/____

HOW OLD MY KIDS ARE TODAY:

WEATHER:

Season: ☐ WINTER ☐ SUMMER ☐ SPRING ☐ FALL

PLACES & SPACES:

List the physical spaces you occupied today (i.e. home, office, grocery store, playground, gym, doctor's office, etc.)

WHAT I WORE:

SOMETHING I'M WONDERING ABOUT TODAY:

THE BEST THING I HELD IN MY HANDS TODAY:

SOMETHING I CHECKED OFF MY TO-DO LIST:

- [ ]
- [ ]
- [ ]
- [ ]
- [ ]
- [ ]

PEOPLE I INTERACTED WITH IN PERSON:

SOMETHING THAT MADE ME LAUGH:

Tiny Spots Of Joy

A Day In The Life

DATE ____/____/____

HOW OLD MY KIDS ARE TODAY:

WEATHER:

Season: ☐ WINTER ☐ SUMMER ☐ SPRING ☐ FALL

PLACES & SPACES:

List the physical spaces you occupied today (i.e. home, office, grocery store, playground, gym, doctor's office, etc.)

WHAT I WORE:

SOMETHING I'M WONDERING ABOUT TODAY:

THE BEST THING I HELD IN MY HANDS TODAY:

SOMETHING I CHECKED OFF MY TO-DO LIST:

- [ ]
- [ ]
- [ ]
- [ ]
- [ ]
- [ ]

PEOPLE I INTERACTED WITH IN PERSON:

SOMETHING THAT MADE ME LAUGH:

Tiny Spots Of Joy

A Day In The Life

DATE ____/____/____

HOW OLD MY KIDS ARE TODAY:

WEATHER:

Season: ☐ WINTER ☐ SUMMER ☐ SPRING ☐ FALL

PLACES & SPACES:

List the physical spaces you occupied today (i.e. home, office, grocery store, playground, gym, doctor's office, etc.)

WHAT I WORE:

SOMETHING I'M WONDERING ABOUT TODAY:

THE BEST THING I HELD IN MY HANDS TODAY:

SOMETHING I CHECKED OFF MY TO-DO LIST:

- ☐
- ☐
- ☐
- ☐
- ☐
- ☐

PEOPLE I INTERACTED WITH IN PERSON:

SOMETHING THAT MADE ME LAUGH:

Tiny Spots Of Joy

A Day In The Life

DATE ___/___/___

HOW OLD MY KIDS ARE TODAY:

WEATHER:

Season: ☐ WINTER ☐ SUMMER ☐ SPRING ☐ FALL

PLACES & SPACES:

List the physical spaces you occupied today (i.e. home, office, grocery store, playground, gym, doctor's office, etc.)

-
-
-
-
-
-
-
-

WHAT I WORE:

SOMETHING I'M WONDERING ABOUT TODAY:

THE BEST THING I HELD IN MY HANDS TODAY:

SOMETHING I CHECKED OFF MY TO-DO LIST:

- [ ]
- [ ]
- [ ]
- [ ]
- [ ]
- [ ]

PEOPLE I INTERACTED WITH IN PERSON:

SOMETHING THAT MADE ME LAUGH:

Tiny Spots Of Joy

A Day In The Life

DATE ____/____/____

HOW OLD MY KIDS ARE TODAY:

WEATHER:

Season: ☐ WINTER ☐ SUMMER ☐ SPRING ☐ FALL

PLACES & SPACES:

List the physical spaces you occupied today (i.e. home, office, grocery store, playground, gym, doctor's office, etc.)

WHAT I WORE:

SOMETHING I'M WONDERING ABOUT TODAY:

THE BEST THING I HELD IN MY HANDS TODAY:

SOMETHING I CHECKED OFF MY TO-DO LIST:

- [ ]
- [ ]
- [ ]
- [ ]
- [ ]
- [ ]

PEOPLE I INTERACTED WITH IN PERSON:

SOMETHING THAT MADE ME LAUGH:

Tiny Spots Of Joy

A Day In The Life

DATE ____/____/____

HOW OLD MY KIDS ARE TODAY:

WEATHER:

Season: ☐ WINTER ☐ SUMMER ☐ SPRING ☐ FALL

PLACES & SPACES:

List the physical spaces you occupied today (i.e. home, office, grocery store, playground, gym, doctor's office, etc.)

WHAT I WORE:

SOMETHING I'M WONDERING ABOUT TODAY:

THE BEST THING I HELD IN MY HANDS TODAY:

SOMETHING I CHECKED OFF MY TO-DO LIST:

- [ ]
- [ ]
- [ ]
- [ ]
- [ ]
- [ ]

PEOPLE I INTERACTED WITH IN PERSON:

SOMETHING THAT MADE ME LAUGH:

Tiny Spots Of Joy

A Day In The Life

DATE ___/___/___

HOW OLD MY KIDS ARE TODAY:

WEATHER:

Season: ☐ WINTER ☐ SUMMER ☐ SPRING ☐ FALL

PLACES & SPACES:

List the physical spaces you occupied today (i.e. home, office, grocery store, playground, gym, doctor's office, etc.)

WHAT I WORE:

SOMETHING I'M WONDERING ABOUT TODAY:

THE BEST THING I HELD IN MY HANDS TODAY:

SOMETHING I CHECKED OFF MY TO-DO LIST:

- [ ]
- [ ]
- [ ]
- [ ]
- [ ]
- [ ]

PEOPLE I INTERACTED WITH IN PERSON:

SOMETHING THAT MADE ME LAUGH:

Tiny Spots Of Joy

A Day In The Life

DATE ____/____/____

HOW OLD MY KIDS ARE TODAY:

WEATHER:

Season: ☐ WINTER ☐ SUMMER ☐ SPRING ☐ FALL

PLACES & SPACES:

List the physical spaces you occupied today (i.e. home, office, grocery store, playground, gym, doctor's office, etc.)

WHAT I WORE:

SOMETHING I'M WONDERING ABOUT TODAY:

THE BEST THING I HELD IN MY HANDS TODAY:

SOMETHING I CHECKED OFF MY TO-DO LIST:

- [ ]
- [ ]
- [ ]
- [ ]
- [ ]
- [ ]

PEOPLE I INTERACTED WITH IN PERSON:

SOMETHING THAT MADE ME LAUGH:

Tiny Spots Of Joy

A Day In The Life

DATE ____/____/____

HOW OLD MY KIDS ARE TODAY:

WEATHER:

Season: ☐ WINTER ☐ SUMMER ☐ SPRING ☐ FALL

PLACES & SPACES:

List the physical spaces you occupied today (i.e. home, office, grocery store, playground, gym, doctor's office, etc.)

WHAT I WORE:

SOMETHING I'M WONDERING ABOUT TODAY:

THE BEST THING I HELD IN MY HANDS TODAY:

SOMETHING I CHECKED OFF MY TO-DO LIST:

- ☐
- ☐
- ☐
- ☐
- ☐
- ☐

PEOPLE I INTERACTED WITH IN PERSON:

SOMETHING THAT MADE ME LAUGH:

Tiny Spots Of Joy

A Day In The Life

DATE ____/____/____

HOW OLD MY KIDS ARE TODAY:

WEATHER:

Season: ☐ WINTER ☐ SUMMER ☐ SPRING ☐ FALL

PLACES & SPACES:

List the physical spaces you occupied today (i.e. home, office, grocery store, playground, gym, doctor's office, etc.)

WHAT I WORE:

SOMETHING I'M WONDERING ABOUT TODAY:

THE BEST THING I HELD IN MY HANDS TODAY:

SOMETHING I CHECKED OFF MY TO-DO LIST:

- [ ]
- [ ]
- [ ]
- [ ]
- [ ]
- [ ]

PEOPLE I INTERACTED WITH IN PERSON:

SOMETHING THAT MADE ME LAUGH:

Tiny Spots Of Joy

A Day In The Life

DATE ____/____/____

HOW OLD MY KIDS ARE TODAY:

WEATHER:

Season: ☐ WINTER ☐ SUMMER ☐ SPRING ☐ FALL

PLACES & SPACES:

List the physical spaces you occupied today (i.e. home, office, grocery store, playground, gym, doctor's office, etc.)

WHAT I WORE:

SOMETHING I'M WONDERING ABOUT TODAY:

THE BEST THING I HELD IN MY HANDS TODAY:

SOMETHING I CHECKED OFF MY TO-DO LIST:

- [ ]
- [ ]
- [ ]
- [ ]
- [ ]
- [ ]

PEOPLE I INTERACTED WITH IN PERSON:

SOMETHING THAT MADE ME LAUGH:

Tiny Spots Of Joy

A Day In The Life

DATE ____/____/____

HOW OLD MY KIDS ARE TODAY:

WEATHER:

Season: ☐ WINTER ☐ SUMMER ☐ SPRING ☐ FALL

PLACES & SPACES:

List the physical spaces you occupied today (i.e. home, office, grocery store, playground, gym, doctor's office, etc.)

WHAT I WORE:

SOMETHING I'M WONDERING ABOUT TODAY:

THE BEST THING I HELD IN MY HANDS TODAY:

SOMETHING I CHECKED OFF MY TO-DO LIST:

- ☐
- ☐
- ☐
- ☐
- ☐
- ☐

PEOPLE I INTERACTED WITH IN PERSON:

SOMETHING THAT MADE ME LAUGH:

Tiny Spots Of Joy

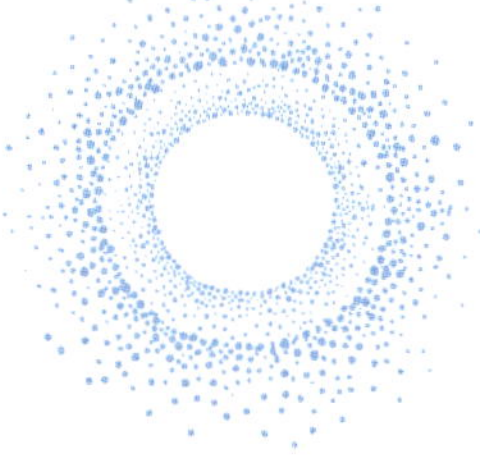

PART TWO

I Want To Remember This

Because those fleeting memories can get fuzzy, faster than you think.

The cute way your toddler lisps "hewwo." The feel of a soft (and often sticky) cheek pressed against yours. Motherhood is full of moments we swear to ourselves we'll never forget as they're happening, but despite our most loving intentions, they do have a way of getting a bit . . . hazy as the years pass.

While we're adamant that nowhere in a mother's job description is "human database," there's something very sweet about being able to tap back into a moment, milestone, or simply an emotion years after it happened—and it's even better when you can correctly identify the kid attached to the memory. Recording memories is truly a "long-game" way of cultivating gratitude, for not just what's happening today, but also for the experiences you've banked in the past.

Luckily, memory-keeping doesn't have to equal regular, long-form journaling—a challenge when time is tight, arms are full, and thoughts and feelings are too big to capture free-form. This structured approach will help you zoom in and jot down just a few sentences that best capture the specific feeling or moment you've just experienced.

How to Use This Section

In this section you'll find 10 prompts. Some of the prompts are poignant, some joyful, some frank, some funny—just like the experience of motherhood. We hope that by capturing what feels like "the same" moment multiple times, you'll begin to notice, and appreciate, what makes each truly unique.

This section is really meant to be used on-the-fly, as quickly after the moment has happened as possible. Be sure to keep this book—and a favorite pen!—nearby, so you can jot down memories as soon as they happen. And, since getting a memory down on paper often inspires longer-form journaling or reflection, we've also included some blank pages near the end of this section for longer entries.

I Want to Remember This

DATE ____/____/____

Conversations With:

WHAT HAPPENED:

HOW I FELT:

-
-
-
-

WHAT I LEARNED:

WHY I'M GRATEFUL:

DATE ____/____/____

I Want to Remember This

Conversations With:

WHAT HAPPENED:

HOW I FELT:

WHAT I LEARNED:

WHY I'M GRATEFUL:

I Want to Remember This

DATE ____/____/____

A Moment of Pure Joy:

WHAT HAPPENED:

HOW I FELT:

WHAT I LEARNED:

WHY I'M GRATEFUL:

DATE ____/____/____

I Want to Remember This

A Moment of Pure Joy:

WHAT HAPPENED:

HOW I FELT:

-
-
-
-

WHAT I LEARNED:

WHY I'M GRATEFUL:

I Want to Remember This

DATE ___/___/___

What a Mess!

WHAT HAPPENED:

HOW I FELT:

WHAT I LEARNED:

WHY I'M GRATEFUL:

DATE ____/____/____

I Want to Remember This

What a Mess!

WHAT HAPPENED:

HOW I FELT:

-
-
-
-

WHAT I LEARNED:

WHY I'M GRATEFUL:

I Want to Remember This

DATE ____/____/____

This Made Me Laugh:

WHAT HAPPENED:

HOW I FELT:

-
-
-
-

WHAT I LEARNED:

WHY I'M GRATEFUL:

DATE ____/____/____

I Want to Remember This

This Made Me Laugh:

WHAT HAPPENED:

HOW I FELT:

WHAT I LEARNED:

WHY I'M GRATEFUL:

I Want to Remember This

DATE ___/___/___

A Lesson I Learned Today:

WHAT HAPPENED:

HOW I FELT:

-
-
-
-

WHAT I LEARNED:

WHY I'M GRATEFUL:

DATE ____/____/____

I Want to Remember This

A Lesson I Learned Today:

WHAT HAPPENED:

HOW I FELT:

WHAT I LEARNED:

WHY I'M GRATEFUL:

I Want to Remember This

DATE ___/___/___

Your Five Sense Memories of Motherhood:

WHAT HAPPENED:

HOW I FELT:

WHAT I LEARNED:

WHY I'M GRATEFUL:

DATE ___/___/___

I Want to Remember This

Your Five Sense Memories of Motherhood:

WHAT HAPPENED:

HOW I FELT:

WHAT I LEARNED:

WHY I'M GRATEFUL:

I Want to Remember This

DATE ___/___/___

I Didn't See This Coming:

WHAT HAPPENED:

HOW I FELT:

-
-
-
-

WHAT I LEARNED:

WHY I'M GRATEFUL:

DATE ___/___/___

I Want to Remember This

I Didn't See This Coming:

WHAT HAPPENED:

HOW I FELT:

-
-
-
-

WHAT I LEARNED:

WHY I'M GRATEFUL:

I Want to Remember This

DATE ___/___/___

A First For ________________:

WHAT HAPPENED:

HOW I FELT:

-
-
-
-

WHAT I LEARNED:

WHY I'M GRATEFUL:

DATE ____/____/____

I Want to Remember This

A First For ______________________:

WHAT HAPPENED:

HOW I FELT:

-
-
-
-

WHAT I LEARNED:

WHY I'M GRATEFUL:

I Want to Remember This

DATE ____/____/____

I Can't Believe This Happened:

WHAT HAPPENED:

HOW I FELT:

WHAT I LEARNED:

WHY I'M GRATEFUL:

DATE ____/____/____

I Want to Remember This

I Can't Believe This Happened:

WHAT HAPPENED:

HOW I FELT:

WHAT I LEARNED:

WHY I'M GRATEFUL:

I Want to Remember This

DATE ___/___/___

I Felt Like a Pro Mom When:

WHAT HAPPENED:

HOW I FELT:

WHAT I LEARNED:

WHY I'M GRATEFUL:

DATE ___/___/___

I Want to Remember This

I Felt Like a Pro Mom When:

WHAT HAPPENED:

HOW I FELT:

-
-
-
-

WHAT I LEARNED:

WHY I'M GRATEFUL:

Notes:

Notes:

Notes:

Notes:

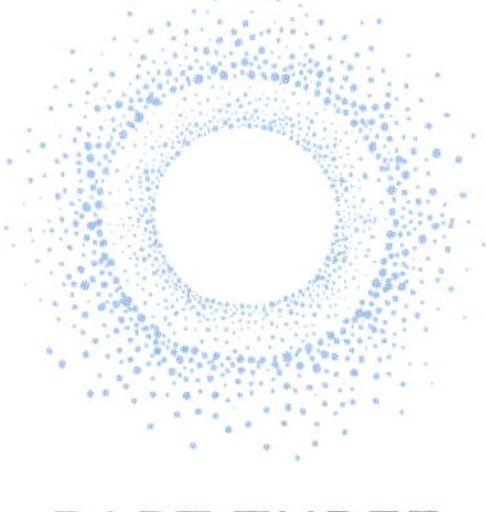

PART THREE

Quick Lists

Capture the essence of where you are in your parenting journey without ever needing to form a complete sentence! (Because let's be honest: some days, that's asking a lot.)

There's so much to love about making a list. When we're bubbling with excitement over a new project, a list helps pin down ideas before they disappear into the ether. When we're feeling unmotivated or overwhelmed, a list can help us prioritize so that inertia doesn't get the best of us. From packing for a trip to shopping for a party, or brainstorming baby names to comparing the pros and cons of a major life decision, list-making gets the stuff of life out of our heads and into a place where we can make sense of it.

At the time of its creation, a list may seem like the opposite of a journal entry. One is unemotional, objective, and brief; the other forgiving in its embrace of both wordiness and sentimentality. But if you've ever happened upon a years-old grocery list in a forgotten notebook or found a crumpled Post-It with must-do tasks from a decade ago, you've probably experienced this truth: lists tell a story of what we're thinking about, planning, and doing.

When the daily details of motherhood are all around us, they seem unremarkable. But someday the specific color of a sippy cup straw or the first few chords of a song will recall an entire universe. Taking note of them today in the form of a little list is one way to honor the world you're building for your family in this season—and to preserve these busy days as a memory for your future self.

How to Use This Section

In this section you'll find 24 prompts for "quick lists." These are themed reflections designed to be done quickly, without thinking too much.

As with the rest of this journal, we encourage you to flip through to find a page that matches up with your mood, situation, or season of motherhood, rather than working through them in order. You'll find some lists that lean into the here-and-now of your physical reality, and others that nudge you to look inward at your emotional experience. In either case, make your lists without overthinking—jot down the first things that come to mind!

Quick Lists

DATE ___/___/___

Smells That Define Life Right Now:

1 ______

2 ______

3 ______

4 ______

5 ______

6 ______

7 ______

Your relationship with your child is more important than the struggles between you.

DATE ___/___/___

Quick Lists

Ways Motherhood Is Getting Easier:

1 ____________________

2 ____________________

3 ____________________

4 ____________________

5 ____________________

6 ____________________

7 ____________________

8 ____________________

9 ____________________

10 ____________________

Quick Lists

DATE ____/____/____

Items I Found in My Bag This Week:

1 ____________

2 ____________

3 ____________

4 ____________

5 ____________

6 ____________

7 ____________

8 ____________

DATE ____/____/____

Quick Lists

Some of ____________'s Favorite Foods:

1 ______________________________

____

____

____

2 ______________________________

____

____

____

3 ______________________________

____

____

____

4 ______________________________

____

____

____

5 ______________________________

____

____

____

MY FAVORITE FOODS AS A KID:

Quick Lists

DATE ____/____/____

Parenting Decisions I'm So Glad I Made:

1 ______________________________

2 ______________________________

3 ______________________________

All children are different, and so are all parents. It's okay to do things your way.

DATE ____/____/____

Quick Lists

Things I Never Thought I'd Say (But Totally Said):

1

2

3

4

5

Quick Lists

DATE ____/____/____

Moments That Make Me Feel Overwhelmed:

1 ____________________

3 ____________________

2 ____________________

4 ____________________

DATE ___/___/___

Quick Lists

Memories I Have from When I Was ____________'s Age:

1

2

3

4

5

6

Seek the balance between acknowledging the hard parts of parenting, and celebrating the joys.

Quick Lists

DATE ____/____/____

Parenting Tasks I Won't Have to Do Forever:

1 ______________________________

2 ______________________________

3 ______________________________

4 ______________________________

5 ______________________________

6 ______________________________

7 ______________________________

8 ______________________________

9 ______________________________

10 ______________________________

DATE ___/___/___

Quick Lists

Snacks Our Family Can't Live Without:

1 ______

2 ______

3 ______

4 ______

5 ______

6 ______

7 ______

Parenting trends come and go, trusting your instincts is timeless.

Quick Lists

DATE ____/____/____

Things in My Grocery Cart / Order Every Time:

1 ______

2 ______

3 ______

4 ______

5 ______

6 ______

7 ______

8 ______

DATE ____/____/____

Quick Lists

Pieces of Pop Culture I Consumed Yesterday (And What I Think About Them):

1 ______________________________

2 ______________________________

3 ______________________________

The experience of motherhood is made up of small moments. Notice the details of your mom-life today.

Quick Lists

DATE ____/____/____

Things I Wear First When the Laundry Is Clean:

1 ____________________

2 ____________________

3 ____________________

4 ____________________

When you're deep in a parenting struggle, ask yourself: Will this matter in a week? A month? A year?

DATE ____/____/____

Quick Lists

Things We Ate This Summer / Fall / Holiday Season:

SUMMER:

1 ____________________
____
2 ____________________
____
3 ____________________
____
4 ____________________
____
5 ____________________
____
6 ____________________
____
7 ____________________
____
8 ____________________
____
9 ____________________
____
10 ____________________
____

FALL:

1 ____________________
____
2 ____________________
____
3 ____________________
____
4 ____________________
____
5 ____________________
____
6 ____________________
____
7 ____________________
____
8 ____________________
____
9 ____________________
____
10 ____________________
____

HOLIDAYS:

1 ____________________
____
2 ____________________
____
3 ____________________
____
4 ____________________
____
5 ____________________
____
6 ____________________
____
7 ____________________
____
8 ____________________
____
9 ____________________
____
10 ____________________
____

Quick Lists

DATE ____/____/____

Things I'm Looking Forward To:

1

2

3

4

5

DATE ____/____/____

Quick Lists

Sounds That Drive Me up the Wall:

1 ______________________________

2 ______________________________

3 ______________________________

4 ______________________________

You are not alone. No matter what you're going through, another mom has been there— or still is.

Quick Lists

DATE ___/___/___

Other Moms I Admire (And Why):

1 ______________________________

WHY:

2 ______________________________

WHY:

3 ______________________________

WHY:

DATE ____/____/____

Quick Lists

The Grossest Parts of Motherhood:

1 ______________________________

____

2 ______________________________

____

3 ______________________________

____

4 ______________________________

____

5 ______________________________

____

6 ______________________________

____

7 ______________________________

____

8 ______________________________

____

9 ______________________________

____

10 ______________________________

____

You are already the mother your child needs most. Let that be enough for today.

Quick Lists

DATE ____/____/____

Vacations I'd Love to Take Someday:

1 ____________________

2 ____________________

3 ____________________

4 ____________________

5 ____________________

6 ____________________

MY IDEAL VACATION DAY:

DATE ___/___/___

Quick Lists

Ingredients for a Perfect Morning:

1 ______

2 ______

3 ______

4 ______

5 ______

You get to decide what you want your family life to look like, and you have the right to change your mind.

Quick Lists

DATE ____/____/____

Things I Love about This Stage of Parenting:

1 ________________

2 ________________

3 ________________

4 ________________

Other people's opinions about your parenting may feel daunting, but in the end, only your opinion matters.

DATE ___/___/___

Quick Lists

(Specific!) Things I See from Where I Sit Right Now:

1 ______________________

____

____

2 ______________________

____

____

3 ______________________

____

____

4 ______________________

____

____

5 ______________________

____

____

6 ______________________

____

____

7 ______________________

____

DETAILS:

Quick Lists

DATE ____/____/____

Things I'd Do with a Completely Free Afternoon:

1 ______________________________

2 ______________________________

3 ______________________________

4 ______________________________

5 ______________________________

6 ______________________________

7 ______________________________

8 ______________________________

9 ______________________________

DATE ___/___/___

Quick Lists

Ways My Friends Make Mom-Life Easier & More Fun

1 ______

2 ______

3 ______

4 ______

5 ______

6 ______

7 ______

8 ______

Close your eyes.
Take a deep breath.
Say to yourself:
It's all going
to be okay.

Notes:

Notes:

Notes:

Notes:

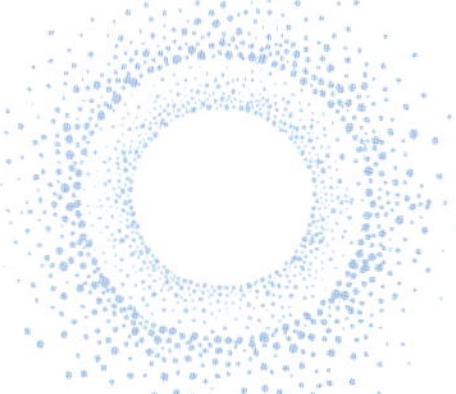

About the Authors

MEAGAN FRANCIS and SARAH POWERS are cocreators of the beloved weekly parenting podcast, *The Mom Hour*. In continuous publication since 2015, and with more than 700 episodes and over 20 million downloads, *The Mom Hour* has connected parents from all over the world to a message they're desperate to hear: It's all going to be OK. Between them, Meagan and Sarah have eight kids from little to grown, and they often approach things with a markedly different set of life experiences, personalities, and parenting styles.

Through thoughtful, nuanced, uplifting, and often funny conversations on their podcast, blog, and social media channels, Meagan and Sarah have created a unique space in the parenting media landscape where there is no one right way to be a great mom—and a ton of different ways to raise great kids. Meagan lives in Southwest Michigan. Sarah lives in Santa Barbara, California.

weldon**owen**

an imprint of Insight Editions
P.O. Box 3088
San Rafael, CA 94912
www.weldonowen.com

CEO Raoul Goff
VP Publisher Roger Shaw
Editorial Director Katie Killebrew
Editor Kayla Belser
VP, Creative Director Chrissy Kwasnik
Art Director Ashley Quackenbush
Senior Designer Stephanie Odeh
VP Manufacturing Alix Nicholaeff
Production Associate Tiffani Patterson
Sr Production Manager, Subsidiary Rights Lina s Palma-Temena

Weldon Owen would also like to thank Kenzie Huff for proofreading.

ISBN: 979-8-88674-132-2

Manufactured in China by Insight Editions
10 9 8 7 6 5 4 3 2

Insight Editions, in association with Roots of Peace, will plant two trees for each tree used in the manufacturing of this book. Roots of Peace is an internationally renowned humanitarian organization dedicated to eradicating land mines worldwide and converting war-torn lands into productive farms and wildlife habitats. Roots of Peace will plant two million fruit and nut trees in Afghanistan and provide farmers there with the skills and support necessary for sustainable land use.